End of Life Care

Ethical and Pastoral Issues

End of Life Care
Ethical and Pastoral Issues

Irish Bishops' Committee for Bioethics

VERITAS

Published by
Veritas Publications
7/8 Lower Abbey Street
Dublin 1
Email publications@veritas.ie
Website www.veritas.ie

ISBN 1 85390 633 6

A catalogue record for this book is available from the British Library.

Design by Colette Dower
Printed in the Republic of Ireland by Betaprint Ltd, Dublin

Veritas books are printed on paper made from the wood pulp of managed forests. For every tree felled, at least one tree is planted, thereby renewing natural resources.

Introduction

Death is a natural part of the human life cycle. It is inevitable and universal. Sometimes it comes suddenly and unexpectedly, like a thief in the night. Sometimes it comes gently at the end of a long and fruitful life. In other cases, however, death is associated with a particular illness, and the struggle to come to terms with death includes the challenge of dealing constructively with the physical and emotional pain both of the person who is dying, and of the people who are close to him or her.

People recognise instinctively that death, however it comes, is the final act in the life of a person, whose dignity must be protected at all costs. We value greatly the fact that somebody has died peacefully, or had a 'good death'.[1] Understandably, both for patients and for their relatives, the possibility of a painful death is something which is perceived as undermining that peace, and also in some sense conflicting with the dignity of the person.

The questions raised by human suffering and dying include questions about why it happens. Questions such as these touch the roots of what it means to be a person.

> The first absolutely certain truth of our life, beyond the fact that we exist, is the inevitability of our death. Given this unsettling fact, the search for a full answer is inescapable. Each of us has both the desire and the duty to know the truth of our own destiny.[2]

Alongside these questions about our ultimate destiny are the practical and ethical questions about how we respond to the physical, spiritual, emotional and social needs of people who are dying, and of those who are closest to them. These are difficult questions which, taking account of the emotions involved, need to be addressed calmly and reasonably, using the resources made available by the Church and the medical profession.

At present there is much debate, both in our own society and elsewhere, about how we ought to care for people at the end of life. Advances in medicine and in

---

technology mean that the taking of decisions about appropriate care for people who have advanced and progressive illness, have become more complex. New terminology and societal shifts add to the confusion many health care professionals feel when faced with clinical decisions pertaining to end of life care.

Unfortunately the discussion on death and dying tends to focus on extremes, and misses out not only on the extensive literature on the experience of people dying, but also on the carer/staff dynamics when relating to patients with physical or mental disability. With regard to the former, there is clear evidence that not only do unacceptable numbers of people die in hospital with inadequate pain relief, but also the political impetus to develop adequate universal palliative care is lacking. With regard to the latter, it would appear that healthcare personnel and carers are, on balance, more likely than unlikely to underestimate the quality of life of those with degenerative and other disabling conditions.

This debate needs to avoid two extremes. Family members and healthcare professionals sometimes refuse to face the reality that people die. They insist on trying to keep the patient alive at all costs, even when it is clear that death is imminent. In situations like this, the patient may even be subjected, by well-intentioned people, to unnecessary suffering or distress. This attitude is sometimes referred to as 'vitalism'. The opposite extreme is when family members, or indeed healthcare professionals, take action to bring about the death of the patient, because they have come to the conclusion that his or her life is no longer worth living. This decision to end the life of a person on health grounds is the essence of euthanasia.

Palliative Care: a realistic and life respecting response to the needs of people who are dying

Palliative care is a relatively new speciality with its origins based in the long tradition of hospice care. Viewing end-of-life decisions from a palliative care perspective may help to clarify some of the issues and outline some of the challenges in providing appropriate care for people at the end of life.

Palliative care avoids extremes in that it both upholds absolute respect for human life and acknowledges human mortality and the limited dominion we have over life. Palliative care is defined as the active total care of patients and their families by a multi-disciplinary team, when the patient's disease is no longer responsive to curative treatment and the focus of care is the quality of life. Palliative care includes consideration of the family's needs before and after the patient's death. Palliative care refers to a philosophy of care rather than a specific building or service and is applicable in all care settings.

Care of patients at the end of life is a continuum of palliative care and usually refers to the final hours or days. This focus on improving and maintaining the quality of a patient's life until the end is life affirming for the patient but also accepting of the inevitability, however unwelcome, of death. Palliative care embraces the principles of non-maleficence (not to harm deliberately) and beneficence (to do good), which are basic ethical principles in all health care practice.

Hospice and specialist palliative care services aim to promote comprehensive care for those with advanced disease and a short life expectancy. It is a matter of maximising the quality of life remaining, while enabling patients to 'live until they die'. While traditionally associated with death resulting from cancer, it is critically important that palliative care services are developed for the many who die from non-malignant disease, i.e. cardiovascular, neurological, and respiratory disease.

Euthanasia: a decision to end life

For the purposes of this document, the following definitions will be taken as understood:

- 'Active Euthanasia' – is where death is caused by a deliberate action. The clear intent is to terminate life.

- 'Passive Euthanasia' – occurs when death is produced by withholding or withdrawing ordinary means of nutrition or treatment for the patients condition with the intention of hastening death.

- 'Voluntary Euthanasia' – is that which is requested by the subject or agreed by him/her when proposed by others.

- 'Involuntary Euthanasia' – is where the agreement of the subject could be sought but is not.

- 'Non-voluntary Euthanasia' – is where the subject is unable to indicate a rational agreement.

Apart from the Netherlands, euthanasia is against the law in Europe and is classed as a criminal act. In Holland euthanasia means the termination of a life by a doctor at the express and voluntary wish of a patient. Since the Dutch Supreme Court declared in 1984 that voluntary euthanasia is acceptable, the law allows a standard defence from doctors if they have adhered to clearly defined official guidelines and conditions. The recent reforms to articles 293 and 294 of the Dutch Criminal Code (10/4/01) have formulated what they refer to as 'the due care considerations' so that when a physician is ending a life he/she must:

- Be convinced that the patient's request was voluntary, well considered and lasting.
- Be convinced that the patient was facing unremitting and unbearable suffering.
- Have informed the patient about their diagnosis and prognosis.
- Have reached the firm conclusion with the patient that there was no reasonable alternative solution.
- Have consulted at least one other independent physician who has examined the patient and formed a judgement about the above points.
- Terminate the life in a medically appropriate fashion.

Under this new legislation, it is not a condition that the patient is dying or that the suffering is physical. Citizens from other countries are not eligible for euthanasia in Holland. As a matter of public policy, other European countries do not allow euthanasia even if the patient wants to die. The victim's consent does not, for instance, provide a defence here in Ireland. Therefore active euthanasia would normally leave anyone assisting liable to the charge of murder.

The Principle of Double Effect

Establishing clear and unambiguous definitions of what does or does not constitute euthanasia is very important in helping healthcare professionals to determine their practice. If a doctor or a nurse equates his/her practice with passive or even active euthanasia due to a poor understanding or definition of terms, then he/she will not be able to differentiate between appropriate clinical practice and euthanasia.

Confusion can arise, in particular, when drugs are prescribed to treat the symptoms associated with the process of dying. Strong pain medication (opioids) or sedatives may be needed to ensure that the patient's dying is relatively pain-free and peaceful. Here the clear intent is to relieve distress, and the possible shortening of a person's life as a result of sedation or respiratory depression, is a secondary effect. Appropriate pain relief or sedation need not necessarily shorten life, but even if in some instances it does, the relief of a distressing symptom may be more likely to enhance life. Healthcare professionals are ethically required to do the most positive good for the patients entrusted to their care and must avoid at all times causing them injury or harm. Good palliative care clearly has a great deal to offer the patient in pain or the patient who is frightened and anxious. Responding to a patient's needs in a holistic manner may in itself prove to be an adequate response to a request for euthanasia.

The principle of 'Double Effect' is an important one and needs clarification. The consequences of an action are important, and they are always morally relevant when they are foreseeable. But consequences alone do not determine the morality of an action. The nature of the action itself (what is being done), and the intention of the person who acts, also influence the moral value of the action. In order for an action to be justified under the principle of Double Effect,

- the act itself (in this case, the relief of pain) must not be intrinsically bad
- the agent must have the right intention – he/she must intend the good effect not the bad
- the good effect must not be achieved through the bad effect

- there must be a proportionate reason to justify the bad effect (i.e., there must not be more harm done than good achieved)

Like other well established moral principles, the Principle of Double Effect is firmly rooted in practical reason and common sense. It is not about splitting hairs. Indeed a good example of it is in the decision that is made to allocate public funds to healthcare. This has the good effect of healing and the relief of pain, but it is not possible without the negative effect of imposing taxation on people, for some of whom at least it may be quite burdensome. The role of government is to ensure that the good effect is actually achieved, and that the negative effect is not out of proportion to the good.

Understanding and Responding Constructively to the Request for Euthanasia

It is well known that the request for euthanasia from the patient with advanced and progressive disease is often transient and may coincide with a bad period of symptom control, even a clinically treatable depression. The findings of a recent study indicated that the desire for death changed with improved pain management and psychosocial support.[3] The study also indicated that depression emerged as the only predictor of the desire for euthanasia. It appears that pain may increase the risk of depression, while increased psychosocial support protects against it.

Where the request for euthanasia persists despite good symptom control, psychosocial, and spiritual care, the challenge to palliative care is to identify and respond to the suffering of the person. Suffering and the response to suffering can in itself have value and meaning to the person. In the study referred to above patients who reported a serious desire for death during the initial stages of the study differed from the rest of the group on the dimensions of pain, family support and depression, including a much higher prevalence of diagnosed depressive disorders. Good palliative care may reduce the request for euthanasia but some patients will want to end their struggle against serious illness in their own way and at a time of their choosing.

The Autonomy of the Patient

For some patients euthanasia will be seen as the ultimate expression of autonomy in that they determine the time and the mode of their dying. Culturally, the prevailing interpretation of autonomy is closely linked to the right to pursue self-interest. This interpretation suggests that there should be no external limits on our own life plans and life goals. Therefore by extension we should have the right to self-determine when we die and how we die.

Autonomy is not absolute. We are not morally justified in doing something simply because we wish to do it. Some decisions that we may be capable of making and carrying out are never morally justified. Among these, for instance, would be the decision directly to destroy an innocent human life. It is, therefore, necessary, especially in formulating legal and medical codes, to balance the desires of the patient who may wish to die with the interests and obligations of society as a whole. To weaken society's prohibition on killing as a response to a small number of individual cases would not be in the best interests of society as a whole. The prohibition on killing is a corner stone of law and social relationships. It protects each of us impartially, embodying the belief that all are equal. Any changes in the legal prohibition on euthanasia would lead to further erosion whether by design, by inadvertence or by the human tendency to test the limits of any regulation. This erosion of protection may impact most on those who are vulnerable and lead to the 'slippery slope' scenario whereby the elderly, chronic sick or disabled may feel pressure, either real or imagined, to seek an early death.

Arguments in favour of euthanasia for elderly patients who have developed dementia are also made. Ironically this occurs at a time when the literature of medical ethics is coming to terms with the societal tendency to undervalue personhood in dementia. Promoting the concept that our personhood is very much more than our cognitive function will require a significant effort. This is a different clinical situation in that these patients are chronically ill, not terminally ill, and they may not be able to voice their wishes coherently. The request for euthanasia may come from a distressed spouse or close relative who feels that the person they knew and loved has already died and that maintaining physical life is of no value. The fact that a patient is no longer competent to make decisions means that he/she risks being reduced to the level of an object to whom things are done. For all that our experience of the person is one of disintegration; of a breakdown in the relationship between the mind, the emotions, and the body, there remains beneath the surface a unique human individual. For this reason particular care needs to be exercised to ensure that decisions are made in a way which takes account of the patient as a whole, rather than viewing him or her from one limited perspective. These situations are very difficult and if euthanasia were permitted it would mean the introduction of a qualitative judgement on what is determined to be a worthwhile life or existence. This would have an enormous effect on the ethos of healthcare provision in this country and it is an area fraught with danger in terms of a potential for abuse and the message it sends out to vulnerable people.

Physician-Assisted Suicide and The Ethos of Medicine

'Right To Die' organisations frequently see suicide as the first step on the road to legalising active voluntary euthanasia. The argument that is used strongly to support assisted suicide is that life has value only so long as it has meaning for the person whose life it is and respect for 'self determination' and 'personal autonomy' should entitle a competent person to decide for himself whether, when and how he/she chooses to end their life. The slogan 'Right To Die' has an appealing sound to it but few expressions are more poorly understood or are more misleading. The failure of such advocacy groups to realise that the greatest risks at the end of life are more likely to relate to inadequate services rather than over-intensive treatment yet again points to the need to ensure that education in ethics has a sound grounding in the evidence base of interventions and prejudice at the end of life.

In general when the expression 'Right To Die' is used people are usually seeking to establish a number of quite distinct claims, which are expressed in terms of the right:

• to reject or to determine unwanted medical procedures including life saving treatment.
• to commit suicide

- to obtain another's help in committing suicide, often subtitled a 'physician assisted suicide', where doctors are the ones to administer the lethal dose or injection.
- to an active voluntary euthanasia, i.e. to authorise someone to kill you intentionally and directly.

While the first of these four possibilities can certainly be regarded as a right, because there is a reasonable balance between the benefits and the risks involved, this cannot be said of the other three possibilities.

At present the legal position regarding 'Right to Die' cases or cases involving withdrawal of life support systems is unclear. Whilst the law recognises a person's right to refuse medical treatment it also recognises that each case is individual and it is very difficult to legislate for all possible situations that may arise. Assisted suicide takes place when another person provides assistance but the suicident commits the last act himself. This is different from active voluntary euthanasia where a person other than the one who dies performs the last act. There is a great deal of literature on the legal issues and the morality of assisted suicide and it is clear that the line between assisted suicide and voluntary euthanasia is often extremely blurred and frequently obliterated.

Medicine and healthcare generally can be seen to have a number of concrete objectives. Among these are the eradication of disease, the relief of pain, the saving of life, and the restoration of health. We must look beneath these objectives for the ultimate purpose of healthcare, which is the well-being of the patient, not just as a body, or as a subject of emotions or of physical sensations, but as a whole person. At times, when the different objectives may even appear to conflict with one another, this requires a degree of balancing. In caring for persons in a holistic way, and especially those who are weak or vulnerable, healthcare professionals are the agents not only of the patient and of his/her family, but also of society. When we say that they are agents, however, that should not be taken to mean that they are mere functionaries who have no right to make decisions in respect of the kind of service they provide. Like their patients, healthcare professionals have a right and a duty to choose what is good, and to reject any course of action which conflicts with an informed judgement of conscience, even if this is requested by the patient or by the family. The legalisation of euthanasia, whether active or passive, would fundamentally alter society's perception of healthcare professionals as people whose whole ethos is rooted in respect for life.

Health care professionals should respect the wishes and values of patients, aiming to enhance the personal autonomy and sense of self worth. Regard for the autonomy of the individual cannot require health care professionals to honour requests for euthanasia given the harm to society and to health care professionals which could ensue. The reality is that even in the Netherlands where euthanasia is permitted and legal sanctions have been removed, only a very small minority of patients uses these methods. The majority of these are patients suffering from cancer and the major factors motivating these requests are depression and severe psychological anxiety. If anything, this tends to lend support to the view that providing better pain control, and better emotional and spiritual support may indeed reduce the interest in and demand for either euthanasia or physician assisted suicide.

The Link Between Physical pain and Emotional Distress

The reason why patients may request euthanasia often go deeper than their physical pain and discomfort from symptoms. Patients may have fears about loss of control, loss of independence and their concerns about the effect of their illness on their loved ones. Sometimes the issue of autonomy and having the right to choose the time, the place, and the method of dying reflects a sense of having lost control over one's life.

It is challenging to be confronted with a person's request for euthanasia when it is persistent and rational. These requests are often couched in terms of the futility of their existence, a loss of meaning and weariness with life. Sometimes the effect of the patient's prolonged dying on family and friends can be the catalyst for the request. It is sometimes argued that for this individual, euthanasia is the only response that will allow them to achieve a good death.

One response in these very difficult situations where the person is clearly beginning to die, is to offer increased sedation to treat the anxiety the patient is experiencing.

The term 'sedation' derived from the Latin *sedare* (to calm), is widely used in anaesthesia and intensive care to describe pharmacological methods used to reduce the awareness of a patient in a state of pain or anxiety.[4] In palliative care, sedation may be defined as the prescription of psychotropic agents with a view to controlling physical symptoms (pain, dyspnoea), psychological symptoms (insomnia, anxiety crises, agitation) or to make the patient unconscious in dramatic situations (sudden haemorrhage).

Even in circumstances such as these, sedation (or an increase in the level of sedation) should not be an automatic choice. Sedation reduces the capacity of the patient to respond freely and deliberately to what is happening in his/her life. If there is an effective alternative which allows the patient a greater degree of consciousness and freedom, such as discovering and responding to the causes of the patient's distress, this would be preferable to sedation. Often patients who are given the option of having more sedation will prefer not to be sleepy and will choose not to have more sedation.

In the last days of life patients and their families are faced not only with physical symptoms, but also with life-cycle changes and role reallocation brought about by the patient's imminent death. Counselling can be particularly valuable to those most vulnerable of patients who have no social support other than that provided by the multi-disciplinary team. Given that there appears to be a link between improved pain management, additional psychosocial support and a reduction in requests for euthanasia, it is vital that counselling is offered to these patients as part of good palliative care.

Palliative care places great emphasis on good communication by the professional team with patients and families and on setting realistic goals for treatment. Talking to people about dying is one of the most challenging aspects of health care, especially when patients seek hope and reassurance. When patients have a better appreciation of the nature of their illness, it is possible to explore their concerns and wishes in a realistic manner. The counsellor/healthcare professional may then address issues of fear, anxiety, loss of control and loss of independence with the patient. Patients who are dying can experience a loss of dignity, a fear of what dying will be like. Counselling allows the patient, the family, and others who are closely involved to discuss these fears. Illness can bring multiple losses to patients and their loved ones, which may change over time. Beliefs and perceptions about certain illnesses may influence the way in which the patient or the family responds to these losses.

Good palliative care encourages open communication between the patient and his/her loved ones. Conflict may arise in situations where collusion is evident, i.e. 'where a group of people agree to keep information from or to misinform others'.[5] The health-professional's training and experience (whether doctor, nurse, social-worker, or chaplain) can help him or her to explore these complex issues with the patient and their families, and liase with the medical team. Palliative care includes consideration of the family's needs before and after the patient's death. The counsellor will negotiate issues of confidentiality, autonomy and consent as part of this process.

The Control of Pain

From the perspective of the patient, the guarantee that pain can be kept within reasonable bounds is an important part of the argument in favour of life and against euthanasia. The patient can be assured that euthanasia is not just morally repugnant, but totally unnecessary. This guarantee can only really be offered to patients who are dying if adequate resources are specifically allocated to palliative care, both in general hospitals and in the community. The inadequacy of such resources impinges directly on the quality of care that can be provided to those who are dying, and may be a contributory factor in the level of demand for euthanasia.

More attention should also be given to the development of a palliative care culture in healthcare generally. Palliative care should not be seen as the sole preserve of palliative care specialists. When this does happen, other healthcare specialists may be deskilled, and patients and their families feel that they are disenfranchised if the do not have access to a palliative care specialist.

Advance care directives/living wills

Advance care directives may take a number of different forms:

- A Living Will – this is a document directing that certain measures should or more likely should not be taken if one is no longer capable of making a rational decision, or incompetent and ill in some specified ways.

- An Enduring Power of Attorney – a document appointing a specific agent who takes specific kinds of decisions and specifies circumstances where one has become incompetent.

- A patient indicates a 'Value history' – the sense of values and what gives their life meaning. It is quite common now to see a combination of all three types of directives drawn together in a formal statement and in some parts of the world, particularly in the United States, patients have constitutional rights to have these directives honoured.

In practice, while there is widespread social acceptance of the idea of advance care directives, there remains considerable reluctance to actually implement them. Problems that have surfaced include the fact that these directives do not necessarily improve communication between patients and their families about the sort of care they would like at the end of life.

A person's view of what constitutes appropriate intervention or withdrawal of treatment may change as the illness progresses. Therefore it is not uncommon to see someone in the whole of their health decide that they would not wish to have certain interventions, reviewing that decision when they actually become ill, and indicating a preference for a different type of intervention. There is also the possibility that medical advances may overtake directives that are too restrictive. Take the instance where a patient directs that he is not to be resuscitated. He may base this on the fact that at present there is a low survival rate in cases similar to his own or that at present there is a significant risk of brain damage following resuscitation. If then there are significant medical advances in the area of resuscitation this may overtake his previous directive.

In Canada it has become common practice in hospitals and continuing care institutions for patients to write or video their 'Care Wish'. This is then usually reviewed every three months at which time the patient can change their opinion in relation to choice of treatment or proxy choice. In Canada you may also appoint a friend or relation as an enduring power of attorney who may make decisions on your behalf in relation to health matters as well as financial matters. However, it has been found in Canada that patients who have not appointed a power of attorney now have 'trustees' appointed on their behalf. Frequently the trustees are not aware of the patient's specific preferences for treatment and are unable to make informed decisions for patients at the end of life.

In Ireland the enduring power of attorney does not include the possibility of making decisions in relation to medical treatment of a patient. Advance care directives are not legally recognised here in Ireland. Families here have no legal right to decide on treatment for their relative unless the patient is a minor.

Living wills are usually concerned with authorising the cessation of treatment in certain circumstances. A person may not morally make a directive that would authorise action with the intent of bringing life to an end. One may rightly refuse a treatment if the burden and risk of the treatment is seen as outweighing the benefit it promises. This is not the same as refusing treatment because one does not see ones life as worth saving. What is at issue is the burden of the treatment and not the burden of one's life.

The legal and moral difficulties in this area stem from the fact that there is, necessarily, a highly subjective element in weighing the burden and the benefit of various treatment options for the individual patient. Faced with more or less identical situations, two patients may quite morally and reasonably come to opposite conclusions – one regarding the burden of pain, expense, risk, etc., as intolerable, the other quite prepared to accept the risk. Obviously it is the patient, rather than the doctor, who is entitled to weigh these factors and make a decision based on the best possible information available. Information which is accurate and sensitively communicated is an essential element in any participation of the patient in the making of decisions about treatment.

It is clear therefore that while advanced directives may help to indicate a patient's preference about the end of life treatment, they are not without problems and they should be viewed as not just a simple document but more as a complex process that will change over time.

End of Life Care: Ethical and Pastoral Issues

Respect for Life – A Theological Perspective

In our attempt to find answers to the questions which arise in the context of serious illness, both faith and reason can be of help to us. It is not a case of choosing between faith and reason. What characterises the human person is rational nature, and for this reason if for no other, any attempt to answer the fundamental questions about human life and death must be firmly rooted in reason. But to the eyes of faith, the very purpose of that rational nature is to make it possible for us to relate to God in a way that no other creature can. Any attempt to understand human suffering and dying that excludes the dimension of faith will inevitably fall short. Faith and reason are not in conflict one with the other.

Each without the other is impoverished and enfeebled. Deprived of what revelation offers, reason has taken side-tracks which expose it to the danger of losing sight of its final goal. Deprived of reason, faith has stressed feeling and experience, and so run the risk of no longer being a universal proposition.[6]

The attitude of respect for life is not exclusive to people of faith, but it does have roots in faith as well as in reason. The Catholic Church absolutely rejects euthanasia as a response to chronic or serious illness. This rejection is rooted in an understanding of the human person as someone who is called into life by God, and the ultimate meaning of whose life is to be found in relationship with God. This vision of the human person is revealed in Scripture, but it can also be discerned through reason in the spiritual nature of the human person.

God is the Creator, and the author of life. Life is his gift to us, and the taking of life, for whatever reason, constitutes the rejection of that gift. The problem arises when the value of life is measured, not in terms of relationship with God, but in terms of utility, or in terms of pleasure and pain. If it is no longer useful, or if it involves too much pain or inconvenience, then it is no longer regarded as gift. If it is no longer regarded as gift, then it seems acceptable to dispose of it.

We must also acknowledge that a request for euthanasia may have its roots in the perception of the relatives and friends, rather than in the desire of the patient. When a person is seriously ill, and death is near, relatives and friends are often emotionally drained by the experience. When someone says, 'I can't bear to see her suffering', and proposes euthanasia as an alternative, it may be interpreted as an expression of compassion, but it may in reality be a failure to recognise the life of the other as gift, and a fear of journeying with one's relative or friend 'through the valley of darkness'. It may also be related to the fact that relatives and friends have not realised what other options palliative care makes possible, apart from the two extremes of euthanasia on the one hand, and unbearable suffering on the other.

Through his incarnation, Christ shares in the human condition, and this inevitably includes the human experience of death. In his case death is violent, and is preceded by much emotional and physical suffering. The paradox is that, far from negating the value of his life, the death of Jesus on the cross becomes the ultimate expression of love. It is not the intensity of his suffering that gives meaning to his death, but the attitude which he brings to it. In the same way, for the person who is dying, it should not be assumed that life is without meaning, even when there is physical or emotional pain, because much depends on the attitude which is brought to that pain. A decision to terminate human life before it has run its natural course is also a decision to terminate the journey of faith before arriving at the destination.

The death of Jesus on the cross is inextricably linked to his resurrection. In the same way, for a Christian, the true meaning of death and dying can only be understood against the background of the Resurrection. In the light of the Resurrection the experience of dying can be lived differently, precisely because it is not the final chapter in the life story of the person who is dying.

Spiritual and Sacramental Ministry in the Last Days of Life

The human person is a unique combination of body and spirit, neither of which is complete without the other. For that reason, a comprehensive approach to healthcare must take account of the spiritual needs of the patient. 'Spiritual' in this context does not necessarily mean 'religious'. Some people do not identify with organised religion, or think of themselves as religious, but every person is spiritual and has spiritual needs.

For Christians, as indeed for many others, the ultimate meaning of personal existence is to be found in relationship with God. All the key moments of life, including the times of sickness and death, have the capacity to bring this relationship into sharper focus. Conversely, the relationship with God has the capacity to shed light on these key events.

One of the principle obstacles to the spiritual care of those who are dying has always been the inability of patients and relatives to communicate honestly, for fear of upsetting one another. This difficulty is compounded if healthcare professionals themselves are uncomfortable with any reference to death or dying. It was not uncommon in the past for the visit of a priest to be deferred until the last minute for fear that the patient might be upset.

By contrast, the ethos of sensitive but honest communication that is so much a part of palliative care greatly facilitates the spiritual and sacramental care of those who are dying. An essential element of good hospice care is the fact that the patient's questions are welcomed and answered appropriately. Talk of death and dying is not 'taboo'. This means that if people pray with the patient, they can pray more honestly too.

There are three sacraments in particular which may be of help to a person who is dying. The sacrament of the anointing of the sick used to be known as Extreme Unction, or 'the last rites'. It was never intended to be primarily a last moment intervention when all else had failed. Properly understood it is the celebration of Christ's healing presence with the person who is sick. It expresses our conviction that, even in the final stages of illness the patient will be touched and healed by Christ, whether this healing is of body, mind, or spirit. Like Christ, the various members of the palliative care team will not abandon the person who is dying.

In the context of serious illness a patient will almost inevitably be drawn to some kind of review of life. There may be some anxiety about things that have been said or done, or things that remain undone. The sacrament of reconciliation, or confession, is not about adding the burden of guilt to the burden of illness. It fits very well into a review of life, by allowing the patient to entrust his or her life to the compassion of God who understands our limitations and our struggles, and in whom all contradictions are resolved.

In the Eucharist the person who is dying is able to receive the body and blood of Christ, who died and is risen. The Eucharist is God's personal pledge of eternal life to the one who is dying. It is food for the journey, the one which still remains to be completed in this life, and the 'onward connection' from this life to the next. Every effort consistent with the dignity of the patient should be made to facilite the regular reception of the Eucharist by those who are dying. It need only be the tiniest fragment of the host, or the smallest drop of the blood of Christ. If a patient is unable to receive, then it is preferable that the priest or minister should bless him with the host, rather than simply passing by and ignoring him.

Conclusion

Palliative care seeks at all times to respect the integrity, individuality, and unique worth of each person regardless of their ability or their functional status. Palliative care recognises that it may not be possible or appropriate to postpone death but equally that death must not be deliberately hastened. Palliative care places great emphasis on the importance of good communication between patients and professionals. The importance of establishing trust between patients and their healthcare team allows the patients wishes about treatment to be honoured while they are able to inform the professionals caring for them.

The autonomy of the individual is one of the corner stones of medical ethics and good medical practice. There have been welcome shifts in society to allow people increased freedom of expression and to promote a more open debate on the nature of our society. Inevitably there has to be some balancing between individual autonomy and societal needs. Respect for individual autonomy cannot be an absolute value in isolation. Some individuals will inevitably find the prohibition on euthanasia very difficult, but weakening the prohibition on euthanasia would increase the risk to society of potential abuse. The rejection of euthanasia for the individual does however entail society providing an adequate and holistic care for those who are in greatest needs, mainly the elderly, the dying and the disabled.

Notes

1   L. O'Siorain, M. Hogan, S. O'Brien, 'Care for the Dying – experiences and challenges', 1996
2   Pope John Paul II, *Fides et Ratio # 26*
3. cf. H. M. Chochinov et al. 'Desire for Death in the Terminally Ill' in *American Journal of Psychiatry*, 152:8, August 1995.
4   cf. Jean-Claude Fondras, 'Sedation and ethical contradiction' in *European Journal of Palliative Care*, 3:1, 1996.
5. R. D. Laing, 'Collusion' in C. F. Monte, *Beneath the Mask: an introduction to the theories of personality*, 1977.
6   *Fides et Ratio # 48.*